For Syd and Lewis

DRAW WITH ROB

HarperCollins *Children's* Books

First published in paperback in Great Britain by
HarperCollins *Children's Books* in 2021

HarperCollins *Children's Books* is a division of HarperCollins *Publishers* Ltd.
Text and illustrations copyright © Rob Biddulph 2021
The author/illustrator asserts the moral right to
be identified as the author/illustrator of the work.
A CIP catalogue record for this book is available from
the British Library. All rights reserved.

HarperCollins *Publishers* Ltd, 1 London Bridge Street, London SE1 9GF.
HarperCollins *Publishers*, 1st Floor, Watermarque Building,
Ringsend Road, Dublin 4, Ireland

Visit our website at www.harpercollins.co.uk

1 3 5 7 9 8 6 4 2

ISBN: 978-0-00-847900-8
Printed and bound in the UK by
Bell & Bain Ltd.

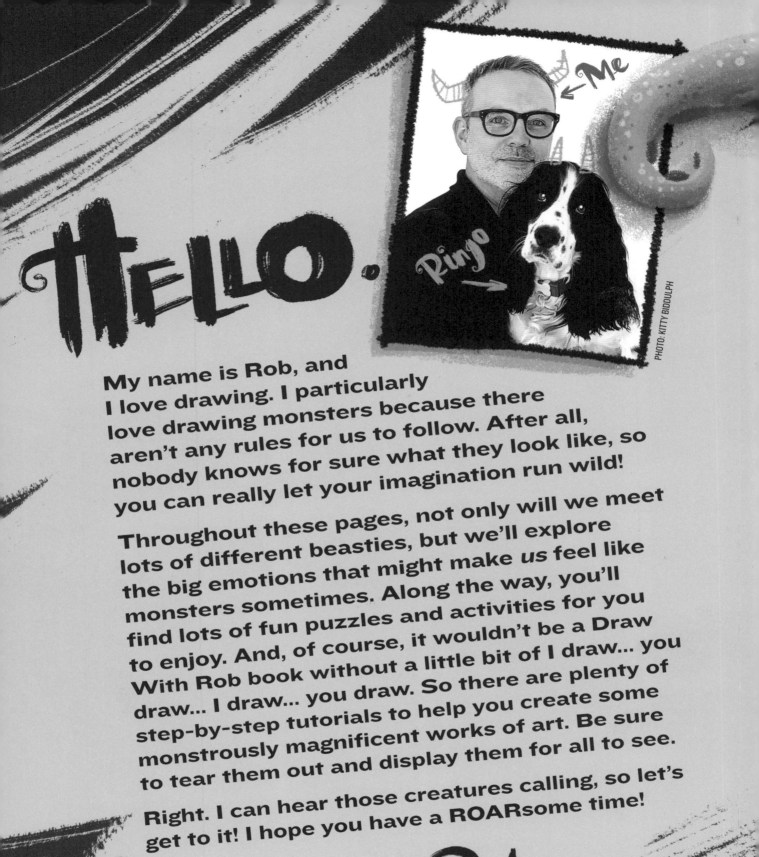

← Me

Ringo →

HELLO.

My name is Rob, and I love drawing. I particularly love drawing monsters because there aren't any rules for us to follow. After all, nobody knows for sure what they look like, so you can really let your imagination run wild!

Throughout these pages, not only will we meet lots of different beasties, but we'll explore the big emotions that might make *us* feel like monsters sometimes. Along the way, you'll find lots of fun puzzles and activities for you to enjoy. And, of course, it wouldn't be a Draw With Rob book without a little bit of I draw... you draw... I draw... you draw. So there are plenty of step-by-step tutorials to help you create some monstrously magnificent works of art. Be sure to tear them out and display them for all to see.

Right. I can hear those creatures calling, so let's get to it! I hope you have a ROARsome time!

Rob x

*Use scissors CAREFULLY

Ask a grown-up for help if you need to!

You will need...

A pencil...

A pencil
sharpener...

A pen...

An eraser...

Something **to** colour with...

and some
scissors.*

Okay,
let's get
started!

THE LAND of MONSTERS

There is a magical place, far from our world, called **The Land of Monsters**. It's where they all come from! They often pop over to visit us, and some even decide to stay. In fact, you'll meet lots of them in this book. But can you find fifteen cheeky monsters hidden here?

ESCAPE from MONSTER MOUNTAIN!

Legend has it that a monster lives in the cave at the top of this mountain. This explorer has stumbled across the monster's lair and needs to escape fast! Can you untangle his ropes and make sure he climbs down the right one?

GRRRRR!

THE WAY BACK DOWN

GRRRRR!

WHO'S HIDING INSIDE?

Draw what you think the monster in the cave might look like. Then turn the page to see if you were right!

the Abominable Snowman

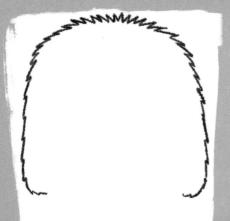

1 Start by drawing a big, upside-down U shape that curves in a bit at the bottom. Make it nice and shaggy all over.

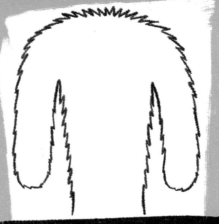

2 Add some more shaggy lines to give your snowman some arms, as you see here. Extend the lines on the inside all the way to the bottom of the page. These will be his legs.

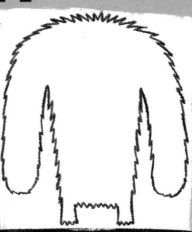

3 Draw two shaggy rectangles at the bottom for feet and join them up in the middle with a straight (but shaggy) line.

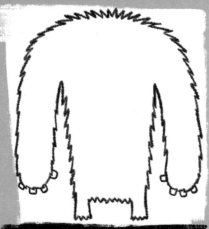

4 Let's give your snowman some fingers – add four little squares with curved edges to the bottom of each arm, just like you see here.

5 It's time for eyebrows. Two tilted rectangles near the top of his head will do the trick.

6 Then add some dots just below the eyebrows; these are the start of your snowman's eyes.

7 Draw a circle around each dot, joined up to the eyebrows, and your snowman can stare right at you menacingly.

8 Draw a line below the eyes for your snowman's mouth. Tilt it down on one side, like you see here, to show how grumpy he is!

9 Finally, draw a zigzag line above his mouth for teeth, and give him some colour. White and blue is nice and icy! Don't forget to add a scribbly shadow underneath.

THE ABOMINABLE SNOWMAN

By.. Age..........

CAN YOU FEEL IT?

Monsters can be scary... and sometimes, so can feelings. **Kevin** and **Sid** are searching for the names of things you can feel in this grid – can you help? Don't forget to tick them off the list as you find them.

Words can run forwards, backwards, diagonally and even upside down!

```
H K M J K W Y D U A N J L M O
H A P P Y B M J F U D N U W G
S D E R A C S O T Q N J E C F
G C D K U G D Y I Z L I X N V
R U J P I F X G Q Y A E C K R
U G Y R G N A L W J V G I L X
M Y Q B H U D V O W M K T D Q
P T C A N E R C R C Y I E Z P
Y F A I M W H S R V A R D O R
C J L V Z E Z H I J O K E L S
U R M S H Y O S E B X P N L A
E S I R P R U S D F U J P H D
P D B N A A V W H T N E V O L
S I Q D W P F M D O K R J M
U L S I B M A D F N G T D
```

Words to find

- [ ] HAPPY
- [ ] SURPRISE
- [ ] KIND
- [ ] ANGRY
- [ ] JOY
- [ ] SHY
- [ ] SAD
- [ ] LOVE
- [ ] BORED
- [ ] WORRIED
- [ ] MAD
- [ ] CALM
- [ ] SCARED
- [ ] GRUMPY
- [ ] EXCITED

Meet the KINDNESS MONSTER

An important part of being kind is understanding and sharing the feelings of others. This is called empathy. **The Kindness Monster** loves being kind and giving hugs – that's why he's so cuddly. Let's turn the page and learn how to draw him...

FUN FACT

Every June we celebrate Empathy Day in the UK. By using characters in books to step into someone else's shoes, scientists say we can train our brains to be more understanding of other people's feelings. Find out more at www.empathylab.uk

the Kindness Monster

1 Let's start with an upside-down **U** shape. Make it nice and shaggy, as I have done here. Then join it up at the bottom with a straight line with two rectangular bumps for the legs.

2 A big curved line right across the middle gives your monster a smiley mouth.

3 Above the mouth, draw two circles and colour them in. Then draw two more circles around the first two. Voila! Our Kindness Monster is awake!

4 Above the eyes, draw two shaggy rectangles tilted upwards for some friendly eyebrows. Add a square with curved edges at each end of the mouth for your monster's teeth.

5 Add two curved rectangular shapes underneath the mouth to give your monster some arms. These should be shaggy too.

6 Draw five rectangular shapes on the end of each arm for fingers, and four on the end of each foot for toes. Colour them all in, just like I have.

7 Let's give your monster some enormous ears – all the better for listening (a very important empathetic skill). Draw a big circle on each side of the head, with another big shaggy circle around it.

8 Finally, it's time for some colour. I've given my monster a heart design right in the middle of his tummy. Be as imaginative as you like, but don't forget the scribbly shadow underneath.

THE KINDNESS MONSTER

By... Age..........

A MONSTROUS MAZE

The gang are having a party, and the **Kindness Monster** is running late. Can you help him find his way through the maze so that he gets there on time?

Way in

Party!

IT'S PARTY TIME!

The monsters are all here, and they're ready to party! Can you colour them in and make sure they have a terrific time?

THE EYES HAVE IT

Monsters are just like people – they come in all shapes and sizes, and you can tell how they're feeling by looking at their eyes. Use your imagination to draw some monsters around these eyes and then see if you can guess how they're feeling.

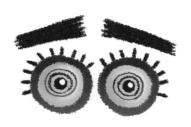

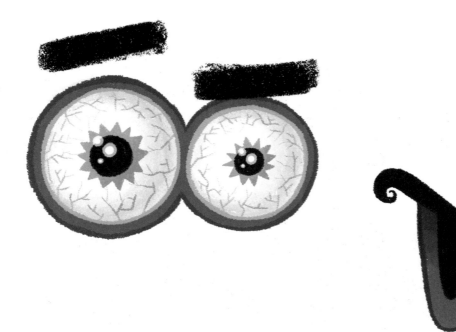

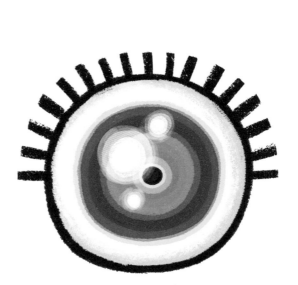

A MONSTER BASH!

Now it's time for you to hold a monster party of your own. Your guests can be real or imaginary, but they'll all need an invitation. There are eight invitations on the following pages for you to tear out and fill in, and there's even space for you to draw a couple yourself. So what are you waiting for? Get party planning!

Please cut out
CAREFULLY

Ask a grown-up for help!

IT'S...
PARTY TIME!

LET'S
CELEBRATE!

PARTY!

PARTY!

PARTY!

Draw your invite here

Dear

You are invited to a
MONSTER PARTY!

It's on

At

Love from

RSVP by

LET THE MONSTER
MADNESS BEGIN!

Dear

You are invited to a
MONSTER PARTY!

It's on

At

Love from

RSVP by

LET THE MONSTER
MADNESS BEGIN!

Dear

You are invited to a
MONSTER PARTY!

It's on

At

Love from

RSVP by

LET THE MONSTER
MADNESS BEGIN!

Dear

You are invited to a
MONSTER PARTY!

It's on

At

Love from

RSVP by

LET THE MONSTER
MADNESS BEGIN!

Draw your invite here

Dear

You are invited to a

MONSTER PARTY!

It's on

At

Love from

RSVP by

LET THE MONSTER MADNESS BEGIN!

Dear

You are invited to a

MONSTER PARTY!

It's on

At

Love from

RSVP by

LET THE MONSTER MADNESS BEGIN!

Dear

You are invited to a

MONSTER PARTY!

It's on

At

Love from

RSVP by

LET THE MONSTER MADNESS BEGIN!

Dear

You are invited to a

MONSTER PARTY!

It's on

At

Love from

RSVP by

LET THE MONSTER MADNESS BEGIN!

THE DARK DOOR

There's something lurking in the dark. Can you spot the six differences between these two pictures? Write what they are in the spaces to the right, and then turn the page to see what's behind the door...

DOCTOR FRANKENSTEIN'S

Doctor Frankenstein is putting his very famous monster (**Frankie**) together, but his lab is such a mess he can't find the pieces. They're hidden somewhere in his laboratory. Can you help him find them all?

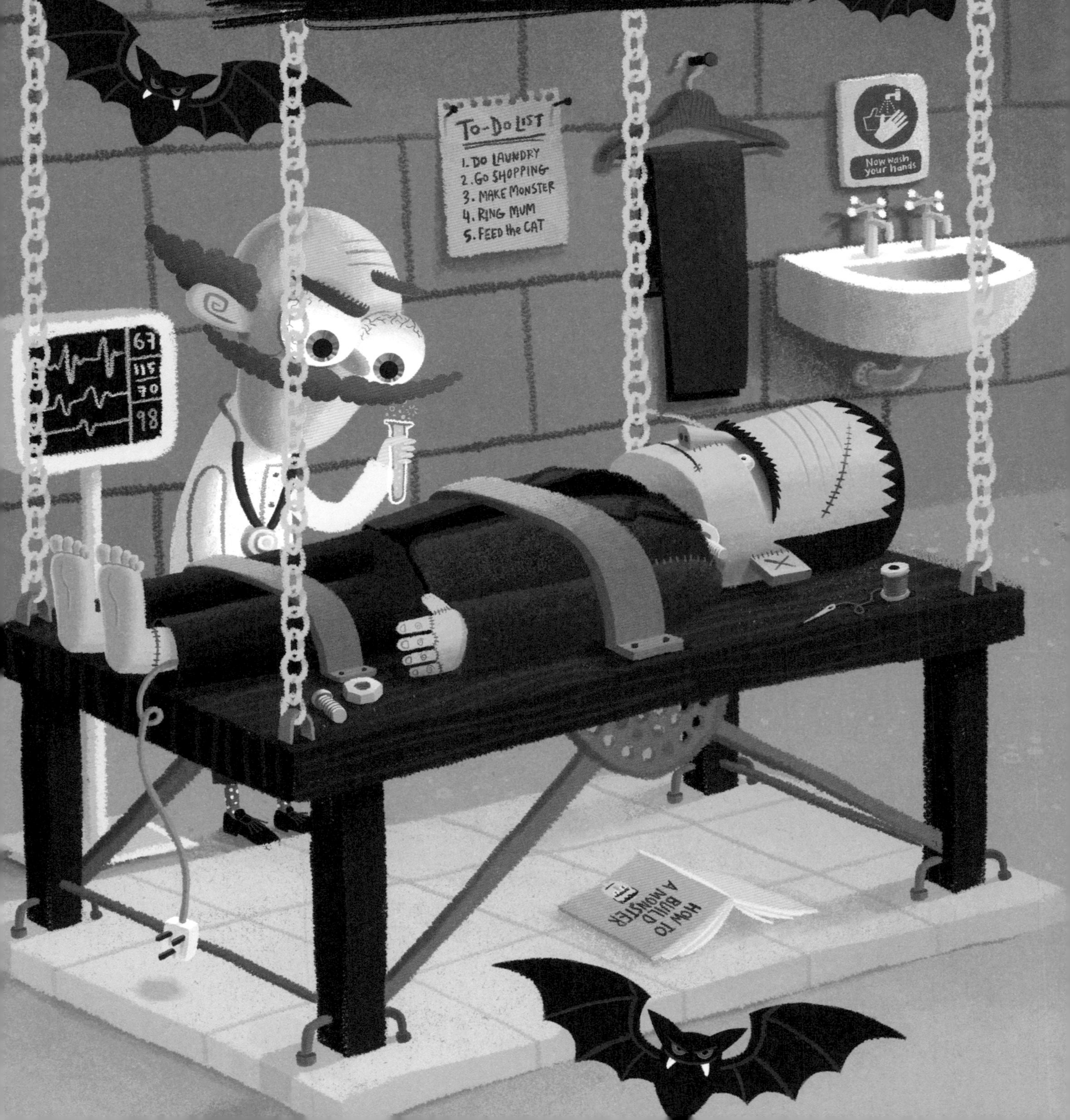

TO-DO LIST

1. DO LAUNDRY
2. GO SHOPPING
3. MAKE MONSTER
4. RING MUM
5. FEED the CAT

Now wash your hands

67
115
70
98

HOW TO BUILD A MONSTER

LABORATORY

15 things to find in this picture

1 Nut and bolt ☐
2 Spare trousers ☐
3 Microscope ☐
4 Spare brain ☐
5 Power cord ☐

6 Nine barmy bats ☐
7 Spare arm ☐
8 Magic potion ☐
9 Needle and thread ☐
10 Heart-rate monitor ☐

11 Nosy werewolf ☐
12 Spare foot ☐
13 Big battery ☐
14 Stethoscope ☐
15 Instruction manual ☐

HOW to DRAW...

Frankie

1 Let's start by drawing a rectangle at the top of the page. Make it a bit wider at the top, and tilt it slightly as I have done here.

2 Add two small squares on each side and draw a big shaggy eyebrow between them. Colour in a zigzagged rectangle at the top of the head too. This is Frankie's hair.

3 Let's give Frankie a face! Add a rectangle for his nose, a dot in a circle on either side for eyes and a curved line underneath for a smile. Add an X in each ear to finish them off.

4 Draw another rectangle underneath his head. That's his neck. Then add two rectangles on each side, for bolts. Make the outside one stripy, as I have done here.

5 Next, draw two rectangles on either side, with triangular shapes as you see here, to make his jacket. Join them up in the middle with two straight lines.

6 Add rectangles on each side for sleeves, and draw little lines to join them to the rest of the jacket like stitches. Then draw a hand coming from the bottom of each sleeve.

7 Two rectangles, joined in the middle, make great trousers! Draw a foot at the bottom of each leg too, with a line of stitches at the ankle to finish them off.

8 Finally, it's time for the finishing touches! I've added scars and a plug as well as colouring Frankie in a nice green. Make sure you add a shadow under his feet.

FRANKIE

By.. Age.............

MONSTROUS ME!

Have you ever felt like a monster? Sometimes big feelings, like being really angry about something, can make you feel like one. Draw what you think you would look like as an angry monster here, and then turn the page to draw **Fiery Red**, MY angry monster.

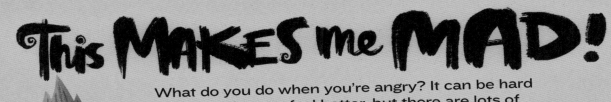

This MAKES me MAD!

What do you do when you're angry? It can be hard to know how to feel better, but there are lots of different things that can help. I have added some below – but can you think of any more?

1 TAKE FIVE DEEP BREATHS

2 TALK TO A FRIEND

3 DO TEN STAR JUMPS

4 COUNT BACKWARDS FROM TWENTY

5 Add your own here

How to Draw... Fiery Red

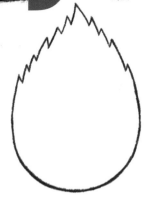

1 First, draw a great big U shape, just like the one I have drawn here.

2 Next, add a point at the top with spiky sides. Looks fiery already, doesn't it?

3 Let's give Red some angry eyebrows. Two pointy wings coming out from the middle will do it! Colour them in, and make the tops spiky as well.

4 Draw a mouth for Red like I have here, by adding a pointy line off to one side and two little triangles for teeth.

5 Some coloured-in circles underneath his eyebrows will make great pupils.

6 Next, draw a circle around them to finish off those two angry eyes.

7 Add a thick zigzag shape on each side of your monster for some arms. Four little pointy bits on each end will make great fingers.

8 Now for the legs. Some bent rectangular shapes will do it, with spiky bits on the end for his toes.

9 Last of all, draw a scribbly shadow underneath and give Fiery Red some colour. Red was perfect for me, but you can use whatever colours you like.

FIERY RED

MAKING a MONSTER

Monsters come in all shapes and sizes. They can be furry, scaly, have tentacles, great big teeth or anything in between! I have drawn parts of some monsters here to get you started. Use your imagination to make them as monstrous as you can.

HOW to DRAW...
the
Loch Ness Monster

1 Start this monster by drawing two long rectangular shapes at the top of the page. Draw a small rectangle on top of each, and then one more about halfway down. Add some little dots, as I have, to give it some detail.

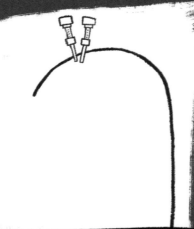

2 Next, draw a big curved line that goes all the way down to the bottom of your page on the right hand side.

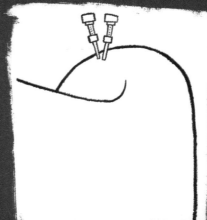

3 On the left end of this curved line, draw a horizontal line with a flick up at the end, as you see here.

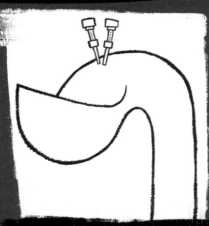

4 From the left end of that line, swoop down and then back up in a nice smooth curve. Then head back down again. This gives your monster a lovely long neck.

5 It's time for some eyes! Draw two circles with lines across the middle, and then add a dot under each line. Finally, draw two tilted lines above the circles for eyebrows.

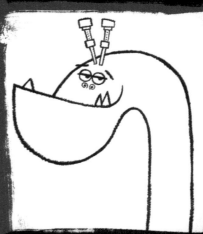

6 Two small spirals just underneath the eyes will be your monster's nostrils. Then add some pointy teeth just as I have here.

7 Draw eight semicircular shapes running down your monster's back to make plates, and we're almost done.

8 In between each plate, draw a triangle down to make a zigzag pattern on your monster's neck.

9 Finally, let's colour Nessie in! You have my permission to use any colours and patterns you want.

THE LOCH NESS MONSTER

By.. Age..........

A LOCH MESS

Nessie is lost in the rivers that feed into Loch Ness. She's desperate to get home where someone special is waiting for her. Can you help her get there?

welcome to
LOCH NESS

WHAT LIES BENEATH?

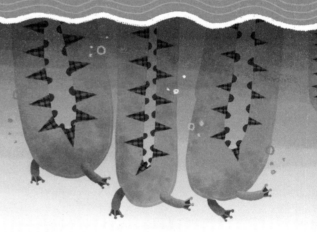

Nessie and **Little Nessie** aren't the only creatures swimming in these waters. Use your imagination to draw them some monstrous friends to play with.

LOST and FOUND

Sometimes when monsters visit our world, they accidentally leave things behind. Our furry (and scaly) friends have left some toys in **Dave**'s bedroom and need to find them before they can go back home. Can you help?

15 things to find in this picture

1 A teddy bear ☐
2 A spotty monster ☐
3 Two yellow socks ☐
4 The Jack of Hearts ☐
5 A penguin ☐

6 A pair of glasses ☐
7 Some crayons ☐
8 Two clawed feet ☐
9 A robot ☐
10 A yellow football ☐

11 Two drumsticks ☐
12 A yellow submarine ☐
13 A glass of water ☐
14 A monster's tail ☐
15 A Draw With Rob book ☐

the Monster Under the Bed

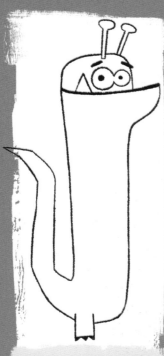

1 Let's start with something easy. At the top of the page, draw a thin rectangle with a knobbly bit on the end.

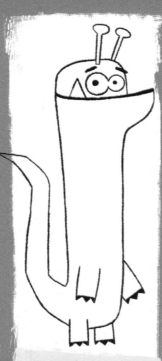

2 Underneath that, draw an upside-down U shape with a line along the bottom that extends out to the right – like a baseball cap.

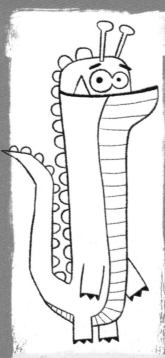

3 Next, draw a line down from the left side of that shape and then curve it up into a long pointy tail, just as I have done here.

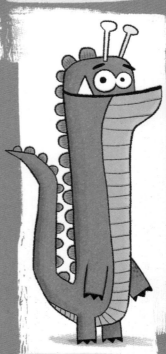

4 From the right-hand side of the baseball cap, draw a long curved line that swoops to the left at the bottom. Draw a rectangular shape in the middle and add three points on the bottom for claws.

5 Back up to the top! Add two circles with dots in the middle for eyes (one bigger than the other), two lines for eyebrows and a big triangle on the left for a tooth. Add a second knobbly antenna too.

6 Give your monster two rectangular shapes for arms, and a second leg behind the first one. Give all of them three pointy claws on the end.

7 Your monster needs some plates. Add lots of semicircles down his back and tail, all the way to the end. Give him a stripy belly too, like you see here.

8 Finally, draw a scribbly shadow under your monster and get colouring! Be as imaginative as you can – anything goes!

Draw with Rob

The MONSTER UNDER the BED

By.. Age............

SLUMBER PARTY

These furry friends have had an exciting night of sleepover fun and are now fast asleep. All except one, that is. Can you spot our wide-awake pal pretending to snooze?

SWEET DREAMS

Monsters dream just like you and me. Good ones, bad ones, silly ones and scary ones. Why don't you draw what this one is dreaming of?

Sleepy Green

1 Draw a big shaggy circle right in the middle of the page.

2 Two U shapes near the top will be your sleepy monster's closed eyes...

3 And an enormous curved line below them gives your monster a lovely sleepy smile.

4 Draw two thin rectangles down from the bottom of your shaggy circle. Add two rounded rectangles on the bottom for feet.

5 Add a rectangular shape on each side for arms, with a zigzag end on each one.

6 A curved point on the end of each foot gives your monster some nice spiky claws!

7 Draw four points on the end of each arm for little claws on the hands too.

8 Time for some horns. Draw two big curved shapes with points on the end, one on each side of your monster's head, just like you see here.

9 Finally, it's time to colour. Don't forget to draw a scribbly shadow underneath your monster, and add a nice speech bubble so Sleepy Green can finally catch some ZZZZZs...

SLEEPY GREEN

By... Age..........

Do the MONSTER MaTcH

Cut out the cards on the following pages and match them in different ways to make the **coolest creatures** you can. The cards are split in to tops, middles and bottoms, and there are even some blank ones on which you can draw your own monsters. So get matching and see what you can come up with...

Please cut out
CAREFULLY

Ask a grown-up for help!

Draw your monster here

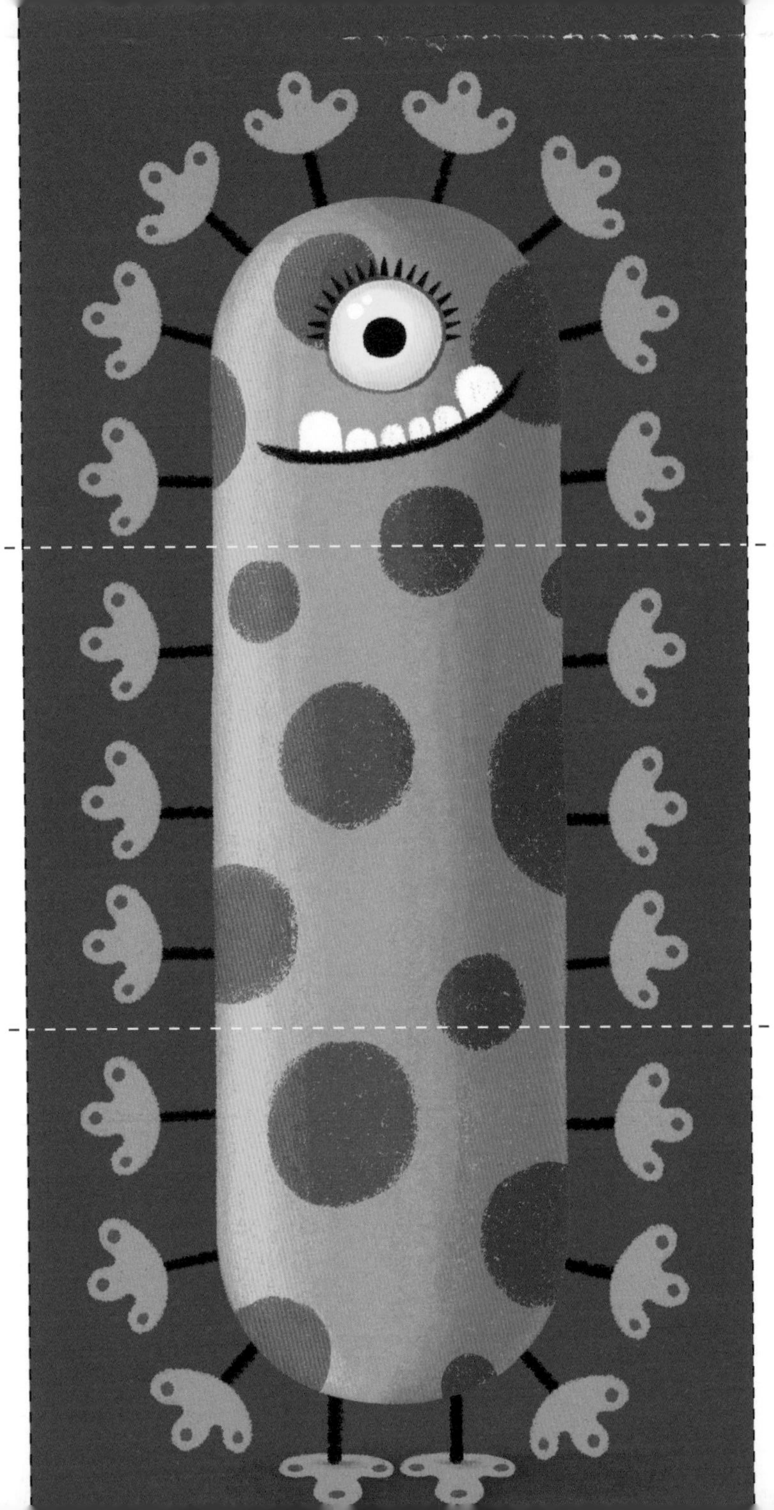

Draw your monster here

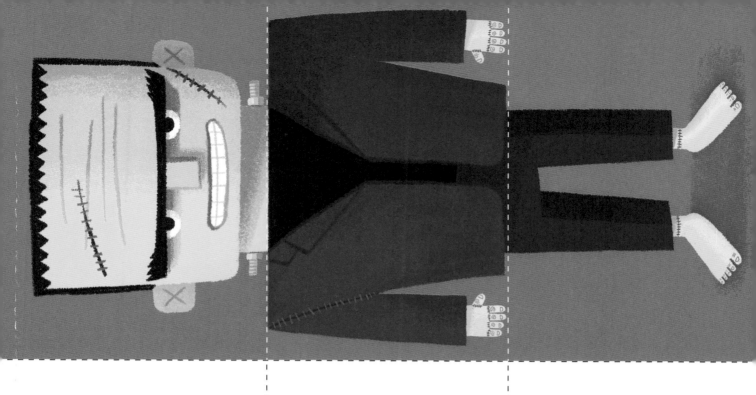

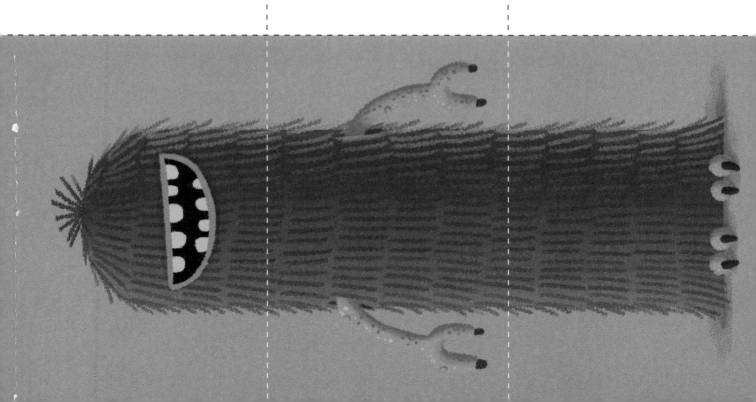

Draw your monster here

Draw your monster here

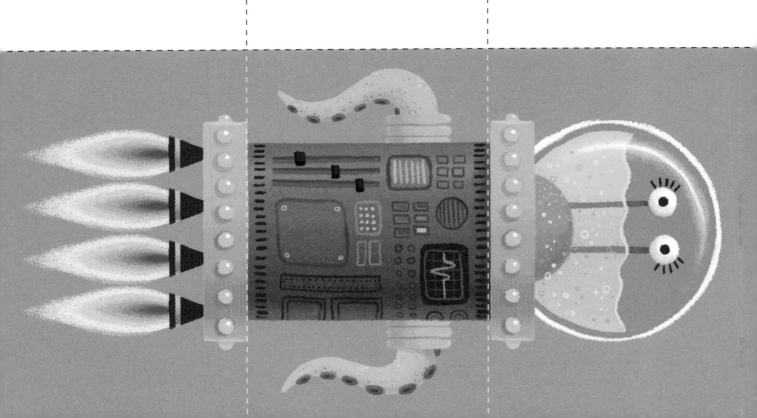

DANCE the FRIGHT AWAY

Your favourite matched-up monsters have gone to the monster party. Can you draw them dancing here?

WORRY BALLO

Everyone carries worries around with them, even monsters. If I have worries, I imagine blowing them into a balloon and then letting them drift away into the sky. These four monsters are very happy to have let their worry balloons go. Can you spot which ones were theirs?

WHAT To Do WITH WORRIES

There are lots of different things that can help you to let go of your worry balloon. Here are some of my ideas, but can you add your own?

Talk to a friend or grown-up.
Keep your hands busy. Drawing can help!
Dance around to some music you like.

Pick up an object that reminds you of a favourite place (for example, a shell from the beach). Close your eyes and imagine how you felt when you were there.

Add your own idea here

How to DRAW...
Blinky Yellow

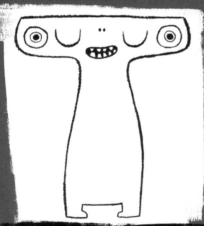

1 Let's start by drawing the outline of a big capital **T** shape at the top of the page, but leave the bottom of the shape open.

2 Extend the two lines to the bottom of the page, and then add two feet just like I have done here.

3 Back up to the top now. Draw a circle at each end of your capital **T**, with a big dot and another smaller circle inside it. Next to those, draw a **U** shape like I have here.

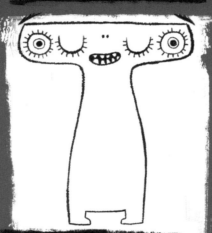

4 Add two tiny dots for nostrils in the middle. Underneath that, draw a curved sausage shape filled with teeth for a big monstery grin!

5 Give all four of your monster's eyes some eyelashes. Then add some eyebrows by drawing a shaggy tilted line above each end of the **T** shape.

6 Draw two curved rectangular shapes inside your monster's body, for arms.

7 Add five little bumps on the end of each arm for our monster's fingers, and then add some more to the inside of each foot for the toes.

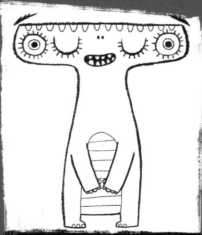

8 Draw an upside-down **U** shape inside your monster's body, and finish it off by filling it with horizontal lines. Then add some stripes along the top of the head.

9 Last but not least, colour your monster in and draw a shadow underneath. Use your imagination to make it as bright and as blinky as possible!

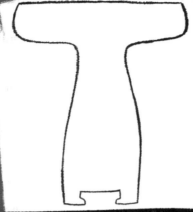
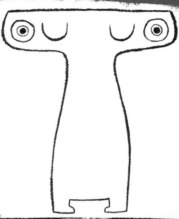

BLINKY YELLOW

By .... Age ....

A The Aquarium

1
Booky
Blue

D The Greenhouse

MERRY MONSTER MATCH

Everyone has different worries, but we all have different things that make us happy too. Can you match these cheerful monsters up with their happy places?

2
Orange
Surfer

3
Aqua
Fintail

B The Bookcase

4
Leafzilla

C The Beach

Ozzy

1 To start, draw an oval on its side, but with pointed ends like a rugby ball. Make the line along the bottom side a bit thicker.

2 Give your monster some eyes by drawing two adjoining circles, like I have here. Add a black dot in each surrounded by another circle. Add two lines on top for eyebrows.

3 Draw two spikes coming up from that bottom line, one on each side of the eyes. These are our monster's pointy teeth.

4 Next, draw two slim, knobbly shapes, and two stripy horns, like I have here. Then draw a shaggy curved shape on the left for an arm.

5 Let's give Ozzy a guitar! Draw the body in the middle like I have, and then a long rectangular shape over to the right for the neck. Add a smaller rectangle on the end.

6 Ozzy needs a body. Draw a shaggy line down from the right side of his mouth, under the guitar, and back over to the left. Join it up to his mouth on the left side too.

7 Draw a big shaggy rectangle on the right side for his left arm. Two slim rectangles down from the bottom of your monster gives him legs. Give each leg three toes.

8 Let's add some detail. Fill in the middle of the guitar like I have here, and draw lots of little lines all the way up the neck. Don't forget to add the little knobs on the end, to the right.

9 It's finally time to rock! Add guitar strings, a scribbly shadow under your monster's feet, and colour him in with your most rock'n'roll colours. Awesome!

OZZY

By.. Age............

WHAT MAKES

ME HAPPY

Now we know what makes our monster friends smile, but what helps **you** find your happiness? Use this space to draw whatever it is. Then turn the page, because me and my monster friends have something to say...

This is to certify that

·····························

is officially a

MONSTER ARTIST

·····························
Date

Rob Biddulph
···························
President of drawing stuff

GOODBYE!

Well done on reaching the end of this monster book! I hope you've had as much fun drawing pictures and making monsters as I have, and I hope that you keep on using your imagination. I certainly will, and you can see the results by reading my stories in these books...

And don't forget to watch all of my **#DrawWithRob** videos on my YouTube channel and follow me on social media

@RobBiddulph   @rbiddulph   RobBiddulphAuthor   Rob Biddulph   @RobBiddulph

www.robbiddulph.com

ANSWERS

THE LAND OF MONSTERS

ESCAPE FROM MONSTER MOUNTAIN

CAN YOU FEEL IT?

A MONSTROUS MAZE

THE DARK DOOR
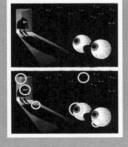

DOCTOR FRANKENSTEIN'S LABORATORY

A LOCH MESS

LOST AND FOUND

SLUMBER PARTY

WORRY BALLOONS

MONSTER OF ROCK
Guitars 3 & 5 are identical

MERRY MONSTER MATCH